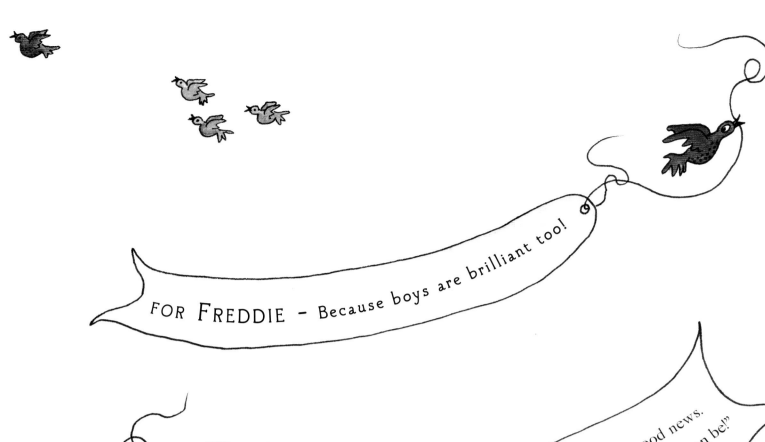

FOR FREDDIE – Because boys are brilliant too!

"Everyone has inside of him a piece of good news. The good news is that you don't know how great you can be!"
ANNE FRANK

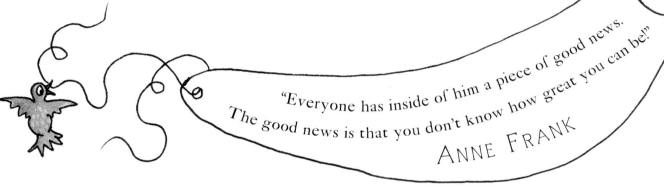

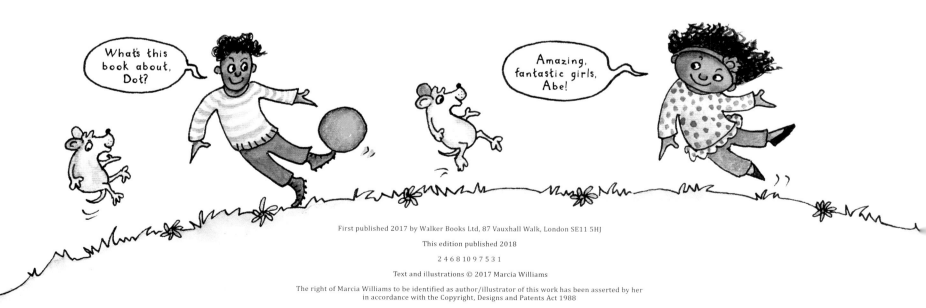

What's this book about, Dot?

Amazing, fantastic girls, Abe!

First published 2017 by Walker Books Ltd, 87 Vauxhall Walk, London SE11 5HJ

This edition published 2018

2 4 6 8 10 9 7 5 3 1

Text and illustrations © 2017 Marcia Williams

The right of Marcia Williams to be identified as author/illustrator of this work has been asserted by her in accordance with the Copyright, Designs and Patents Act 1988

This book has been typeset in Caslon Book

Printed in China

British Cataloguing in Publication Data is available

ISBN 978-1-4063-7997-6

www.walker.co.uk

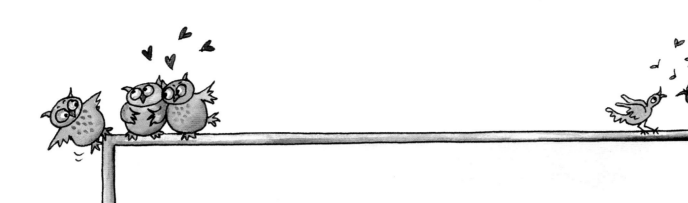

THREE CHEERS FOR WOMEN!

WRITTEN & ILLUSTRATED BY

MARCIA WILLIAMS

Boys do amazing, fantastic things too!

Of course they do. But there are lots of books about them already!

WALKER BOOKS
AND SUBSIDIARIES
LONDON • BOSTON • SYDNEY • AUCKLAND

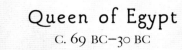

CLEOPATRA VII

Queen of Egypt

c. 69 BC–30 BC

Cleo may not have been a great beauty, but she had charm.

Cleo spoke seven languages.

Her little brother was no real match for her cunning and ambition!

If Caesar hadn't loved Cleo he might have conquered Egypt.

I rule Egypt, but I only speak Greek.

Just learn to say "please", Dad!

Cleopatra's father was Pharaoh Ptolemy XII of Egypt. His family was originally from Greece, but they had ruled Egypt for over 200 years.

What do you know about Egyptian culture, Dad?

Not a lot, Cleo.

Cleopatra was really smart and became the first of her family to speak Egyptian. Her father adored her and taught her all he knew about ruling Egypt.

OK, so Dad's dead and I'll do the ruling.

Not for long, sister!

When Cleopatra was eighteen years old she inherited her father's throne with her brother, Ptolemy XIII – he was only ten years old.

You're a little squirt, you know nothing about ruling!

I'm a boy, I do the ruling.

In Egypt women were supposed to come second to men but Cleopatra didn't like that idea. She wanted to be the sole ruler of Egypt.

Now you're out and I'm in.

Not for long, brother!

As he grew older her brother Ptolemy objected to this and finally threw Cleopatra out of the palace so he could rule alone.

How can you resist me?

I can't.

Luckily, Julius Caesar, the Roman leader, was visiting Egypt. Cleopatra hid inside a rug and had herself delivered to him – he was captivated!

Never mess with your sister!

Caesar helped Cleopatra to raise an army against Ptolemy. He was no match for the ambitious pair and died at the Battle of the Nile.

Help Dot, I've shrunk!

It's book magic, Abe.

Do you think Cleo loved Caesar?

Probably not!

Cleopatra was Queen of Egypt again! She was very popular and helped Egypt become a rich and successful country.

Cleopatra and Caesar had a son they named Caesarion, but Caesar refused to make him his heir, naming his grandnephew, Octavian, instead.

Caesarion means "Little Caesar".

In 44 BC Caesar was murdered and Cleopatra feared Octavian would invade Egypt.

To protect his future, Cleopatra made Caesarion her co-ruler, but kept the real power herself.

Then she persuaded Mark Antony, one of Rome's new leaders, to join forces with her.

Cleo dressed as the goddess Isis to capture Antony's heart!

Mark Antony fell deeply in love with Cleopatra. The pair challenged Octavian to a battle at sea in 31 BC, but their heavy ships were no match for the Roman vessels and Octavian defeated them.

Cleo feared becoming Octavian's prisoner.

Antony and Cleopatra fled to Egypt, where Antony killed himself after hearing the false news of Cleopatra's death. Heartbroken, Cleopatra dressed in her finest clothes and then allowed a poisonous asp to bite her, so that she would die too.

After Cleopatra's death Octavian made Egypt part of the Roman Empire. So, although Caesarion may have held nominal power for a few days before Octavian had him executed, Cleopatra was the last ever true pharaoh of Egypt.

Cleo was only 39 years old when she died.

Boudicca

Warrior Queen of the Iceni

C. AD 25–61

Boudicca was born in south-east Britain. She lived with her parents until they died when Boudicca was only seven.

Luckily, Boudicca was then adopted by another family.

They sent her to warrior school where she learned to fight.

She was fearless and had fierce eyes that made enemies tremble!

Boudicca grew to be very tall and had beautiful, flowing red hair.

She married Prasutagus, king of the Iceni tribe of eastern England.

They had two daughters together and life was good.

At the time, Britain was under Roman power. They let Prasutagus rule his kingdom but charged taxes.

Then in AD 60 Prasutagus died and the Romans seized his wealth, leaving his family with nothing!

Like me, Boudicca had royal blood.

Boudicca was a Celt - one of the people who lived in Britain before the Romans arrived.

She always seemed destined for greatness.

Not wise to steal from a warrior queen!

8

The Iceni people rebelled, but the Romans were too strong for them. Some Iceni had their homes burned to the ground and others were taken into slavery. Boudicca and her daughters were captured.

Boudicca was outraged! When she was released she rallied other tribes and together they captured three Roman cities. Then they were attacked by the Roman governor and his army of 10,000 men. Boudicca was now leading about 100,000 men, so it seemed as though she would win, but her men weren't trained, and they were already tired and hungry after their recent battles. Boudicca's army was defeated. Boudicca and her daughters poisoned themselves to avoid being captured again. Her rebellion had not succeeded in chasing the Romans from Britain but it did eventually lead to all Celtic tribes getting a fairer deal from the Romans. Boudicca never let the Romans conquer her and she became a symbol to freedom fighters everywhere.

Boudicca was determined to protect her people from the Romans.

Boudicca is also known as Boudicea, Boadicea and Buddug!

Boudicca was defeated by governor Gaius Suetonius Paullinus in AD 60 or 61.

Boudicca was given a burial fit for a hero!

Joan of Arc

Teenage Warrior

C. 1412–1431

"I would rather die than do something which I know to be a sin, or to be against God's will."

The struggle between France and England during 1337-1453 is called the Hundred Years' War.

Run, before they kill us!

I hate the English.

In 1412, when Joan was born in the French village of Domrémy, much of France was under English rule. When Joan was nine years old, her village was raided by English soldiers.

Good morning, pigeons, hens, sheep, pigs and all!

Joan was a quiet, gentle child. She didn't go to school, but worked on her father's farm.

Your turn, Joan.

Sorry, I'm off to church now.

She was very religious and loved going to church, even when her friends wanted her to play!

Joan often heard voices through the notes of the church bells.

Don't be scared, but be a good girl and go often to church.

Oh I will, I do.

When Joan was thirteen years old, she began to hear voices and see visions of saints and angels. Joan grew to love and trust the voices.

You have one year to drive the English into the sea.

I will try, but I'm just a peasant girl.

When Joan was sixteen St Michael, St Catherine and St Margaret appeared to her. They told Joan to drive the English out of France. Joan believed it was God's will.

Joan liked to take the bell ringer little presents.

I am God's messenger and you are the true King of France.

She cannot be serious!

Is she God's messenger or a crazy peasant?

Dressed in boy's clothes, Joan went to the French ruler, the Dauphin Charles. He laughed at her! But his soldiers continued losing to the English.

She is sent by God.

Eventually, Joan was given a suit of armour and command of the French army. Awed by their leader, the soldiers went into battle with renewed hope.

Because Joan believed the voices came from God she felt bound to obey them.

Why did Joan dress as a boy?

Her voices told her to.

She was incredibly brave.

Led by Joan, the French army drove the English from the city of Orléans, and then from smaller towns close by.

Afterwards they marched to Rheims, where Charles was crowned King of France! Joan was now ready to go home, but the king ordered her to fight on.

Then during a battle at Compiègne, Joan was captured by the French traitor the Duke of Burgundy. He sold her to the English and she was imprisoned.

In 1431, after an unfair trial, Joan was found guilty of witchcraft. She was burnt in the marketplace at Rouen at the age of nineteen. King Charles did not lift a finger to rescue the girl who had saved France from the English and won his crown for him! Today the French see Joan of Arc as a national hero and she remains an inspiration to women throughout the world.

Joan led her men into battle brandishing her banner instead of a sword.

She was wounded several times in battle, but always fought on.

Joan could get very angry if her soldiers behaved badly or skipped church.

Pope Benedict XV declared Joan a Saint in 1920.

Elizabeth I
Queen of England, Wales & Ireland
1533–1603

"There shall be but one mistress here, and no master."

Many Tudors, including Henry VIII, believed only men could rule.

Elizabeth's brother, Edward VI, and sister, Mary I, both ruled for a short while before she did.

Elizabeth encouraged writers and artists.

Shakespeare, Ben Jonson and Christopher Marlowe are all Elizabethan writers.

A beautiful daughter!

Take her away, I need a son!

Elizabeth was born in London on 7 September 1533. Her dad, Henry VIII, was not pleased! He wanted a son to inherit his crown.

Dad'll be turning in his grave!

But Henry's only son died, so Elizabeth was crowned in 1558.

My people are my children.

England is my husband.

Parliament wanted Elizabeth to marry, but she politely refused.

If I marry, my husband will get to rule instead of me!

Elizabeth was very clever and wanted to rule the country herself.

Shall we talk in English, French, Italian, Spanish, Greek or Latin?

Um...

I'm fast and furious!

Knock, knock. Who's there?

Sleep tomorrow night, if you must!

Elizabeth spoke six languages. She loved riding, playing music, writing poetry, dancing, flirting and making jokes. She also worked extremely hard, often keeping her ministers up all night!

Dolt!

Gore belly!

Cod's head!

Puh!

Elizabeth was not perfect. She was moody and sometimes spat at or beat servants who displeased her.

Three cheers for good Queen Bess!

We are charmed to meet you!

However, in public Elizabeth was always gracious. She dressed to impress her people and they loved her.

Inheriting a crown doesn't make you great!

It's what you do with it that counts!

Elizabeth increased literacy ...

helped the poor ...

Elizabeth tried hard to avoid wars, but it was impossible. She was a Protestant and some people wanted a Catholic on the throne. Mary Queen of Scots, who was a Catholic, spent nineteen years plotting against her, and in 1588 the Catholic king of Spain sent a fleet of ships called the Armada to invade England. Luckily, aided by a storm, Elizabeth's navy triumphed! Elizabeth rode through the streets in celebration.

Not bad for a girl, eh, Daddy?

Elizabeth didn't have children, so she was the last Tudor monarch. When she died in 1603, the crown passed to King James VI of Scotland, uniting England and Scotland. Henry VIII had left his daughter a troubled nation, but she had made it so strong and prosperous that her reign became known as "The Golden Age".

Luckily, Elizabeth had built up her father's depleted navy.

Elizabeth employed spies who warned her of impending attacks!

Her naval commanders finished their game of bowls before attacking the Spanish.

Elizabeth hated old age. She had all the mirrors removed from her palaces.

proved that women were amazing ...

expanded trade ...

and introduced the first flushing toilets!

Now that really did change the world!

Mary Wollstonecraft

Author & Radical Feminist
1759–1797

"The divine right of husbands, like the divine right of kings, may, it is hoped, in this enlightened age, be contested without danger."

Mary tried to help and protect her mother.

In Mary's time few women had the same education as men.

Women were expected to marry or stay at home.

Mary was like a bird, she wanted to fly free!

Mary was born in London on 27 April 1759. Her childhood was miserable – her mother disliked her and her father was a bully. He also kept moving his family to avoid paying his debts.

Mary was clever and longed to learn history and Latin like her brothers, but girls were only taught needlework and simple sums.

Luckily, when Mary was fifteen she was befriended by her intellectual neighbours, Mr and Mrs Clare, who let her use their library.

Mary wanted to be independent and left home at nineteen to be a lady's companion. Later, she opened a school with her best friend, Fanny.

Fanny eventually married, but Mary didn't believe in marriage. She wanted to stay single and earn her own living.

Sadly, Fanny became ill after the birth of her first child and died. Mary, who had few like-minded friends, was heartbroken.

After Fanny's death and rescuing her sister from a violent marriage, Mary had to give up her school, but was determined to remain independent.

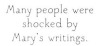

Mary decided to support herself as an author, which was very brave as few women earned an income from writing at this time.

To begin with, Mary worked for a publisher and met many free thinkers like herself, including the poets William Wordsworth and William Blake.

Many people were shocked by Mary's writings.

Mary wrote several books and political pamphlets. The two most famous were *The Vindication of the Rights of Men* and *The Vindication of the Rights of Woman*.

In 1789, drawn by the French Revolution, Mary went to Paris. She fell in love with an American, Gilbert Imlay, and they had a daughter, Fanny.

In France Mary felt less restricted and more able to be herself.

Little Mary later married the poet, Percy Shelley, and wrote *Frankenstein*.

When the relationship collapsed, Mary returned to London with Fanny, and she eventually married the philosopher and writer, William Godwin. Their marriage was very unconventional for the time – William agreed to respect Mary's right to work and to share the household duties with her. They had a daughter, but tragically Mary died eleven days after giving birth – she was only 38 years old. Mary lived during a period when women's voices were rarely listened to, but she had made herself heard! She is now seen as a founder of feminism and her books went on to inspire women to fight for the right to vote.

Feminists want equal rights for women.

Jane Austen

Novelist

1775–1817

"Know your own happiness."

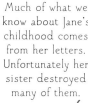

Much of what we know about Jane's childhood comes from her letters. Unfortunately her sister destroyed many of them.

"Our brood!"

Jane

Jane was born in Hampshire, England, on 16 December 1775 to George and Cassandra Austen. She was the seventh of eight children – six boys and two girls.

Jane's father was handsome and clever, her mother was witty and shrewd.

"Latin, boys, is the language of logic."

"Festinare!"

Her father was a clergyman who also tutored young boys.

"We're just like twins, aren't we?"

Jane was a lively little girl and very close to her sister, Cassandra.

"Your papa has no money for the fees, you must leave."

"I'll leave if Cas leaves."

For a while they went to boarding school together.

At this time girls were not encouraged to read novels!

"I'm going to be clever, just like you, Cas."

When they returned home, Jane determined to educate herself.

"I think I could be a writer!"

She read all the books in her father's library.

"Now Chaucer wrote in rhyme royal…"

She also listened hard when he taught his pupils!

Jane often read her stories aloud to her family.

"Oops, ink on the sheets again!"

From an early age, Jane had a passion for writing.

"We love acting in Jane's plays!"

She wrote poems, stories and plays for her family to act out.

"Your observations are so acute, Jane!"

"Oh, Papa!"

Jane had a talent for writing about people in everyday situations.

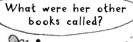

"Jane wrote *Sense and Sensibility*, *P&P* and *Northanger Abbey* by the age of 23!"

"What were her other books called?"

"*Mansfield Park*, *Emma* and *Persuasion*."

Jane often wrote about love but never married. She had a short romance with Tom Lefroy, a young man from Ireland, but he never proposed.

When she was 27, Jane accepted an offer of marriage from a rich landowner. But the very next morning she changed her mind!

Jane never stopped writing. In 1797 her father sent an early version of her novel *Pride and Prejudice* to a publisher, but it was rejected.

Then in 1803, her brother Henry sent an early version of *Northanger Abbey* to a publisher. He said he would publish it but never did!

When Jane's father died, Jane and her sister and mother moved to a cottage on their brother's estate. And in 1811, her first book – *Sense and Sensibility* – was finally published! Jane published three more during her lifetime, all anonymously. It wasn't considered "proper" for ladies to have jobs – or even to have their own opinions! When Jane died aged 41, Henry revealed that she had written the books. Jane's books were very popular during her lifetime and they're even more popular now. She is one of the world's best-loved novelists.

Jane once wrote to her niece telling her not to marry a man she didn't love.

Scary Gothic novels were fashionable at the time.

I'm glad she had her sister for company.

Jane is believed to be the author of over 40 new words: door-bell, sponge-cake and dinner-party ... SNORE!

Florence Nightingale

Nursing Pioneer

1820–1910

"I attribute my success to this: I never gave or took an excuse."

In Victorian England nursing was not a respectable profession, but work for the uneducated.

From an early age Florence had a passion for nursing. She was born into a large, wealthy family, so she had plenty of relations to practise on – as well as all her dolls!

Florence was very clever and excellent at maths.

After a visit to a local hospital, which was squalid and uncaring – as most hospitals were at this time – Florence decided to become a professional nurse.

Her parents did not believe that respectable young women should become nurses, but they finally allowed her to go to Germany for training.

Luckily, her dad believed in educating girls!

Then in March 1854 Britain and France joined the Ottoman Empire in the Crimean War against Russia. British soldiers were rushed into battle.

Florence wanted to help. So the Minister of War asked her to take a team of 38 nurses to the army hospital in Scutari, Turkey.

Dr Hall was worried Florence would send bad reports back to England.

When Florence arrived, Doctor Hall, who was in charge, tried to drive her away. He didn't want her team to see the terrible conditions he'd permitted.

Florence wasn't going anywhere! She and her nurses set about scrubbing the filthy wards, exterminating the rats and making the soldiers more comfortable.

Florence and her nurses also took over the kitchens so that the soldiers had warm and nourishing food.

When winter came and the men had no suitable clothing, Florence brought them warm clothes and blankets.

Doctor Hall continued to make Florence's life difficult, but the other doctors were grateful for her care and the improvement in their patients.

The soldiers loved Florence, as so many of them owed their lives to her. They called her "the Lady with the Lamp" because of her late-night ward rounds.

At the end of the war Florence returned home a hero. Queen Victoria presented her with a gold brooch. Florence used her fame to help improve nursing and sanitation for all. She opened a school for nurses and worked until her death at 90, writing and collecting statistics to prove the importance of hygiene and skilled nurses in preventing the spread of disease. Through her passion, intelligence and determination, Florence changed the face of healthcare for many people, both in England and abroad.

Florence met Mary Seacole, another famous nurse working in the Crimean War.

Florence became known as the Angel of the Crimea.

In Victorian times only the rich had access to healthcare.

Florence used her own money to send trained nurses into workhouses.

Marie has many firsts to her name!

Marie was the first ever woman to receive a PhD from a French university ...

... the first woman to be employed as a professor at the University of Paris ...

... and the first woman to win the Nobel Prize - the most prestigious science prize in the world!

Albert Einstein was a great admirer of Marie.

MARIE CURIE

Physicist & Chemist
1867–1934

"Have no fear of perfection; you'll never reach it."

"We love our children too!"

Marie was born in Warsaw, Poland and was the youngest of five children. She was a bright child. Her parents were both teachers and loved poetry, books and learning.

"We'll look after you, Papa."

When Marie was just ten years old her mother died of tuberculosis.

"Nothing in life is to be feared, Papa. It is only to be understood."

Sad as she was, Marie continued to do brilliantly at school.

"You take my classes today, Marie." "Oh no, Papa, I'm too little!"

Like her father, she was particularly good at maths and physics!

"One day women will be able to attend." "I hope you're right."

But Marie was not able to attend the men-only university in Warsaw, so she and her sister Bronya joined a secret group who held classes for women.

"You go first, you're the eldest." "Can't you swap, she looks more fun!"

Marie also worked as a governess to pay for Bronya to study as a doctor in Paris.

"Mon Dieu, who's going to pick Marie up today?" "She's whiter than a boiled egg!" "Women students!"

When Bronya qualified, she invited Marie to live with her and study in Paris too. Marie had very little money and sometimes she would faint from hunger. But she still completed degrees in physics and maths!

"What would you do if you had Marie's brains?" "Design shoes that helped you do a double backflip!" "How's that going to help your fellow human?"

In 1894, Marie met and fell in love with Pierre Curie, a fellow physicist. The couple married and had two children, Irène and Ève.

Marie and Pierre started working together in a draughty shed, researching radioactivity – the invisible rays given off by certain elements.

They discovered two new elements, polonium and radium. Tragically, in 1906 Pierre was killed in a carriage accident. Heartbroken, Marie carried on their work, winning a second Nobel Prize in Chemistry.

During the First World War, Marie created x-ray machines for ambulances. She and her daughter Irène drove one of these "Little Curies" to the front lines.

Marie had taken over Pierre's teaching post at Sorbonne University in Paris, becoming the first female professor there. After the war she gave lectures around the world, famous as the first person to win the Nobel Prize twice! Her discoveries led to radiation being used to treat diseases such as cancer and inspired many other scientists.

Marie kept a sample of glowing radium next to her bed as a nightlight ...

... she didn't realise the dangers of over-exposure to radiation.

Marie named polonium in honour of her homeland, Poland.

Marie tried to donate her gold Nobel Prize medals to the war effort.

Marie's eldest daughter also won the Nobel Prize for Chemistry.

Eleanor Roosevelt

Human Rights Activist
1884–1962

"You must do the thing you think you cannot do."

Roosevelt means "rose field" in Dutch.

Eleanor was born 20 years after the abolition of slavery in America.

But there was still much social, political and racial inequality.

Eleanor had a passion for hockey at school.

So where is my new daughter?

With the nurse.

Eleanor Roosevelt was born in New York on 11 October 1884, into a wealthy but rather unhappy and distant family.

I don't feel very happy today.

Who cares? I want to party!

Eleanor's father Elliott suffered from depression, which her mother found hard to cope with.

I love you.

You are so plain and solemn, I shall call you Granny!

Eleanor tried to comfort her mother, but her mother was often unkind and found no comfort in Eleanor.

You're a whole half minute late, Papa!

My own darling little Nell.

When Eleanor was eight her mother died, and Eleanor grew very close to her father. She would count the minutes until he returned from work.

Well, don't just stand there, give your grandmama a kiss.

Eleanor was heartbroken when, several months after her mother's death, her father died too. Eleanor went to live with her grandmother, Mary Hall.

Whatever you do you'll be criticized, so always do what you believe to be right, girls!

Oh, I do believe I am happy at last!

Eleanor did not feel at home at her grandmother's, but luckily when she was fifteen her grandmother sent her to school in England. Eleanor blossomed – she made friends, travelled widely and learned to be confident, independent and articulate. She stayed in England for three happy years.

Eleanor said we should fight for people's freedoms every day!

Well, she certainly did that – exhausting!

And she went flying with Amelia Earhart and applied for her own piloting licence.

When Eleanor returned to New York, she was expected to go to parties and find a husband. But Eleanor was more interested in helping poorer people.

Eleanor married her cousin Franklin Roosevelt, who also wanted to improve life for less privileged people. They had six children, one of whom died as a baby.

Franklin called Eleanor "Babs".

And then, in 1933, Franklin became President of the United States of America! Eleanor supported him as First Lady, but continued her fight for social justice. In 1938, at a Human Welfare Conference in Birmingham, Alabama, Eleanor refused to obey the state's segregation laws. When ordered to move out of the African-American seating and into the "Whites Only" section, Eleanor placed her chair exactly midway between the two areas!

Eleanor could only cook scrambled eggs...

But she had an excuse: she was very busy raising money for poor families!

THE UNIVERSAL DECLARATION OF HUMAN RIGHTS

Adopted by the General Assembly of the United Nations in 1948,
the Universal Declaration states basic rights and fundamental freedoms
to which all human beings are entitled.

ALL HUMAN BEINGS ARE BORN FREE AND EQUAL.

EVERYONE IS ENTITLED TO THESE RIGHTS NO MATTER THEIR RACE, RELIGION OR NATIONALITY.

EVERYONE HAS THE RIGHT TO LIFE, LIBERTY AND SECURITY.

Pretty good for a "plain and solemn child"!

Eleanor wrote a newspaper column called "My Day" and she also wrote 27 books!

After Franklin died in 1945, Eleanor represented the USA at the United Nations and helped to draft the Universal Declaration of Human Rights. She was repeatedly voted America's "Most Admired Woman of the Year" for her commitment to the rights of all people, and was active and influential for the rest of her life.

AMELIA EARHART

Pilot
1897–1937

"Women must try to do things as men have tried."

When Amelia Earhart was born in Atchison, Kansas on 24 July 1897, little girls were expected to wear pretty dresses and play quietly with dolls, but Amelia never liked to do either.

Amelia, her sister Muriel and their dog, James Ferocious, all liked adventure. Ferocious chased strangers while the girls built a roller-coaster, tobogganed, cycled and played a scary make-believe game called "Bogie"!

In 1909 the Wright brothers flew one of the first ever aeroplanes around the Statue of Liberty. But Amelia was unimpressed with the rickety planes of the time.

But ten years later Amelia was at a stunt-flying exhibition when a pilot nose-dived towards her. Amelia was hooked on planes from that moment!

During World War I, while visiting family in Canada Amelia met wounded soldiers and immediately left school to become a nurse's aide. Then in 1920 a pilot took her on her first flight, and Amelia knew she had to learn to fly herself.

Amelia started to save towards flying lessons. By 1922 she had her first plane and set her first women's record by flying to an altitude of 14,000 feet.

On 17 June 1928, Amelia became the first woman to fly across the Atlantic. She and her crew returned to New York to a ticker-tape parade.

The first African-American to fly was Bessie Coleman in 1922.

Bessie was a dare-devil, just like Amelia!

Yes, they both liked to challenge the traditional role of women.

I think I'll challenge the role of birds and start walking!

Watch out for cats then!

In 1937 Amelia set out to try to be the first woman to fly around the world. Sadly, Amelia and her navigator, Fred Noonan, disappeared after covering over 22,000 miles of the flight, more than two thirds of the total distance. Nobody knows what happened to them, but Amelia would have felt proud that she had shown that men and women were equal in "jobs requiring intelligence, coordination, speed, coolness and willpower".

Frida Kahlo

Painter

1907–1954

"My painting carries with it the message of pain."

Frida lived and died in the Blue House.

Frida's father encouraged her to get an education.

Her mother wanted her to learn to cook and get married!

Frida's self-portraits were always honest.

Frida Kahlo was born in Coyoacán, Mexico on 6 July 1907. She had five sisters and lived in a house called the Blue House with her German father and her Spanish-Mexican mother.

You must swim, play football and wrestle. Then your leg will get strong!

When Frida was six years old, she caught a disease called polio that left her right leg damaged for life.

Then, when Frida was eighteen, she suffered life-changing injuries in a bus accident.

You can paint.

Frida had to stay in bed for months. Her parents encouraged her to take up painting – they built her a special easel so that she could paint while lying on her back. She painted herself and her school friends.

"I paint my own reality."

Frida was never really strong again. She gave up her dream of becoming a doctor, but continued to paint. Frida started to paint self-portraits that reflected the pain caused by her accident and were influenced by Mexican folk art.

Do you get the feeling you're inside a Frida Kahlo painting?

Yes. Isn't it a good adventure!

It's very colourful, but prickly too.

Frida supported the Mexican revolutionaries who wanted political change. She was never afraid to attend rallies and spoke out against social injustice.

In 1929, Frida married Diego Rivera, a famous muralist. They went to live in America and Frida started to exhibit her work. It received a mixed reception.

Diego and Frida got divorced and then remarried.

Eventually, the couple returned to Mexico, but they had a very difficult relationship and lived separately for long periods.

Frida's work was getting more recognition, but her health was getting worse. In 1950 she spent nine months in hospital, but she never stopped painting.

Frida adapted native Mexican fashion to hide her scars.

In 1953 she had her first solo exhibition in Mexico. She was very ill, so she arrived by ambulance and then held court from a four-poster bed in the gallery!

Frida Kahlo died on 13 July 1954, just after her 47th birthday. Even though she struggled with pain and unhappiness throughout her life, Frida remained strong, determined and honest. We can still see this today in the colourful and beautiful paintings that she left behind to inspire us.

Frida went on her last protest march ten days before her death.

Frida is still seen by many as an icon of female creativity.

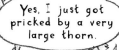

Anne Frank

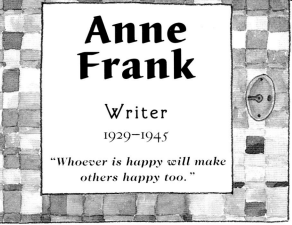

Writer
1929–1945

"Whoever is happy will make others happy too."

In June 1929, in Frankfurt, Germany, a Jewish woman named Edith Frank gave birth to a baby she called Anne. Edith, her husband Otto and their first daughter Margot were all delighted.

Otto and Edith Frank encouraged both their daughters to read.

But in 1933, Adolf Hitler, of the Nazi party, became leader of Germany. Hitler hated Jewish people so the Franks moved to Amsterdam, in the Netherlands.

Hitler tried to turn everyone against the Jews.

Anne was a bright, playful four-year-old and soon learned to speak Dutch. Both she and her sister, Margot, loved their new schools.

Then, in 1939, the Second World War began. A year later Germany invaded the Netherlands. Life became increasingly difficult for Jewish people.

The Jews all had to wear the yellow Star of David.

Anne and Margot had to leave the schools they loved and move to a Jewish school. Otto had to hand over his business to non-Jewish friends.

The family tried to live normally, celebrating special occasions. On Anne's thirteenth birthday, they gave her a diary and she began to write about life under the Nazis.

Jews couldn't use public transport or even sit on benches.

Meanwhile, Otto had prepared a hideout behind a bookcase at his work. Soon after Anne's birthday, fearing arrest, the family moved in.

In order not to arouse suspicion when they moved in, the family had to wear their clothes in layers and just fill a satchel with precious possessions. Anne took her new diary!

The hideout was very small and cramped, especially once another couple, the Van Pels, had moved in with their son, Peter, and their friend, a dentist called Fritz Pfeffer. Forced to remain quiet and indoors, Anne comforted herself by sharing all her teenage thoughts and secrets with her diary. The Franks had good friends outside who supplied them with food, books and other provisions, but after two years they were discovered by the Nazis.

In August 1944 the Germans stormed into the secret hideout and sent everyone to prison camps. Sadly, Anne died of an illness called typhus in early 1945. She was just fifteen years old. Since then millions of people have read her diary, which shows the strength of the human spirit in the midst of unimaginable horror.

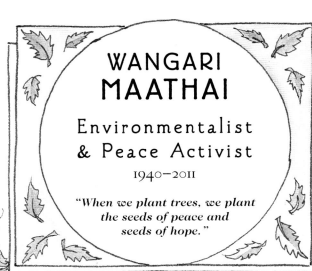

WANGARI MAATHAI

Environmentalist & Peace Activist

1940–2011

"When we plant trees, we plant the seeds of peace and seeds of hope."

In April 1940, a girl named Wangari was born in a small village in Nyeri, Kenya. The village was shaded from the hot African sun by beautiful trees. Wangari grew up listening to the chatter of the birds and animals that shared their forest.

Wangari's father was a farmer.

Good job, Wangari.

From an early age Wangari enjoyed helping her mother to grow and harvest their food.

She also fetched water and caught fish from a nearby stream, which flowed cool and clear.

Then Wangari and her mother would gather firewood and cook together – there was always plenty for all.

Wangari loved the colour of the red Kenyan soil.

Your grandparents' spirits rest in the shade of this tree.

Are you there great grandfather?

When her work was done, Wangari loved to lie in the shade of the trees and listen to her mother's tales about their ancestors.

Girls don't go to school!

Wangari will go!

You heard your mother.

When Wangari was eight years old her parents sent her to school. She worked very hard and in 1960 she won a scholarship to study in America.

When Wangari was a child, few Kenyan girls went to school.

Where are the trees, the shade, the animals, the birdsong?

The loggers came and cut down the trees.

The animals and birds have lost their homes.

Crops won't grow.

I'm hungry.

In America Wangari was awarded a degree in biology, the science of living things. But when she returned home in 1966, Wangari found that many of the living things in Kenya had vanished. Loggers and farmers had cut down millions of trees so the land had become barren. Children were hungry and women had to walk miles for water and firewood.

Hi! No trees means no birds - meet the desert rats.

One person can make a BIG difference!

I'm going to collect a bag of acorns and plant them.

Watch out rats, our days are numbered - the women are planting trees!

"Mama Miti" means "mother of trees" in Swahili.

In 1971 Wangari became the first woman from East Africa to earn a doctorate degree.

Wangari knew that without trees the land becomes desert and crops and animals are unable to thrive. She also realised that as food and water became scarcer, people would become poorer and start fighting over the small amount that remained. So Wangari talked to women all over Kenya. She showed them how to plant and tend to trees. The women could earn some money for keeping the trees alive, and could sell the firewood they didn't need. Thousands of women took up Wangari's challenge; what became known as the Green Belt Movement had begun and little saplings were nurtured all across the land.

On World Environment Day, 1977, Wangari launched her movement by planting seven trees in a Nairobi park.

In 2004 Wangari became the first African woman to be awarded the Nobel Peace Prize for her fight for "sustainable development, democracy and peace". In Kenya the tree is a symbol of peace, so to celebrate her prize Wangari planted a Nandi flame tree at the base of Mount Kenya. At the time of Wangari's death, in 2011, the Green Belt Movement had planted more than 30 million trees and increased the income and independence of countless women. Thanks to Wangari, children in Kenya can once again sit in the shade of a tree and listen to tales of their ancestors.

Wangari was also a political activist, calling for democracy and freedom of expression.

Mae C. Jemison

The First African-American Woman to go into Space

1956–

"Never be limited by other people's limited imaginations."

The first woman in space was Soviet cosmonaut Valentina Tereshkova in 1963.

About 550 people have flown in space. Only 60 of them have been women.

In space, a sneeze can send you flying backwards!

Zero gravity makes a candle flame perfectly round.

Mae Jemison spent her childhood in Chicago and, even when she was in kindergarten, she dreamed of becoming a scientist.

Mae was a stargazer and wouldn't let anyone limit her dreams. She never doubted that she would be one of the first American women astronauts.

But Mae also had other ambitions. She wanted to be a dancer and a doctor! Her mother persuaded her to go to medical school and dance in her spare time.

In 1981 Mae graduated from Cornell Medical College and joined a volunteer group called the Peace Corps. She worked as a doctor in Liberia and Sierra Leone.

After seeing Sally Ride become the first American woman in space, Mae called NASA. Finally, in 1987, she was accepted on to the space programme!

THINGS SPACE SCIENTISTS STUDY:

• Growing vegetables under weightless conditions
• How to make better medicine
• Bone density
• Space sickness

Mae became the first African-American woman to be admitted into the astronaut training programme. After a year of training she earned the title of Science Mission Specialist. This meant that Mae was able to conduct scientific experiments about the effects of weightlessness (or zero gravity) on space shuttle crew.

The shuttle launches like a rocket, orbits like a spacecraft and lands like a plane.

A space shuttle's external tank is just taller than the Statue of Liberty.

"I belong here as much as any speck of stardust."

EXTERNAL TANK

SOLID ROCKET BOOSTER

The crew lives here!

ORBITER – the part that travels to space and back

Space suits are usually worn only during take-off and landing, to protect the astronaut if there is a problem with the air in the shuttle. There is no air in space, so space suits carry a supply. Mae's was orange, so she could be easily spotted by rescuers if she had to parachute from the spacecraft.

READY FOR LAUNCH

MAE IN HER SPACESUIT

In space, water doesn't bubble when it boils and your face swells up.

Astronauts' legs get thinner - they develop bird legs!

Fruit flies, mice, monkeys, chimpanzees, guinea pigs, rabbits, frogs, reptiles and dogs have all gone on space missions!

Another space heroine, Katherine Johnson (1918-), joined NASA in the 1950s as a "computer" - a mathematician. She helped put the first man on the moon!

Mae flew her space mission from 12 to 20 September 1992, on the shuttle *Endeavour*. She took a poster from a dance theatre along with art objects from West African countries on her space mission, to symbolise that space belongs to all nations and all peoples. When Mae looked down from space on Chicago, she imagined the little girl down there that she used to be, and thought that little girl would be "tickled" to see Mae the astronaut! Once back on Earth, Mae decided to leave NASA and develop technology that can help people all over the world in their daily lives. Mae also opened a summer camp for budding young scientists, and encourages everyone to get involved with space exploration, whatever their race, gender or background.

Yes, it looks like an aeroplane toilet!

I love it when people follow their dreams.

Especially when they catch them!

Cathy Freeman

Olympic Hero
1973–

"I enjoy being a woman!"

Cathy loves being both Australian and Aboriginal.

Cathy was born in February 1973 in Queensland, Australia to Aboriginal parents. Aboriginal Australians are the country's indigenous people, who have often been disadvantaged by European settlers.

Cathy, please just walk!

I can't, I'm a runner!

From a young age Cathy knew she wanted to be a runner and showed great talent, but her family had no money for a professional trainer.

Cathy's full name is Catherine Astrid Salome.

"It all comes down to having the confidence to be who you are!"

That's just what I tell my little Roo!

But Cathy was very determined and was just eight years old when she won her first gold medal at a school athletics competition.

Go, girl!

Cathy's stepfather helped her to train. She ran barefoot around and around a grass track.

Cathy's stepfather always believed she'd win an Olympic gold!

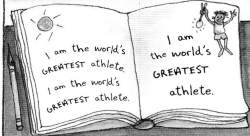

I am the world's GREATEST athlete. I am the world's GREATEST athlete.

I am the world's GREATEST athlete.

Her mother encouraged her to write "I am the world's greatest athlete" over and over again.

Now I'll get the training I need to win an Olympic gold!

When she was thirteen, Cathy became one of a very few Aboriginal children to win a scholarship to boarding school.

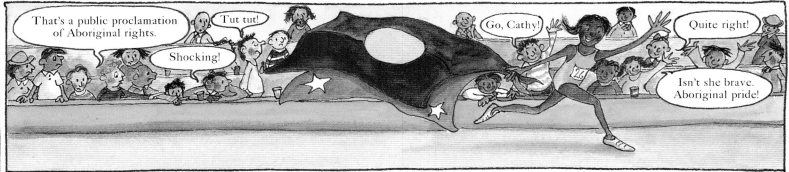

That's a public proclamation of Aboriginal rights.

Tut tut!

Shocking!

Go, Cathy!

Quite right!

Isn't she brave. Aboriginal pride!

A teacher bought Cathy her first proper running shoes.

At just sixteen years old, Cathy won a gold medal at the 1990 Commonwealth Games in the 100 metres relay team. Then in 1994, Cathy won individual gold medals in the 200 and 400 metre races. She ran her lap of honour waving both the Australian flag and the Aboriginal flag, shocking some people but delighting others.

Cathy just followed her dream.

She was amazing!

Do you think she's got the longest and the fastest legs ever?!

Want to hear me laugh, heeeheeeheee!

The first indigenous Australian to win an Olympic medal was Samantha Riley in 1992.

In 1996, Cathy won a silver medal at the Olympics in the 400 metres.

In 1990 Cathy was chosen as the Young Australian of the Year ...

... and in 1998 she was named Australian of the Year!

In 2000, when the Olympics was hosted by Sydney in Australia, Cathy was chosen to light the Olympic flame. Then, to the delight of her home crowd, Cathy went on to win a gold medal in the 400 metres. This time, when Cathy waved both the Aboriginal flag and the flag of Australia the crowd cheered wildly! Cathy Freeman may not have been the first indigenous Australian to win an Olympic medal, but by sharing the pride she has in her roots, she helped to unite a nation and became a symbol of hope for the Aboriginal people. Cathy is now retired from racing, but continues to fight for the rights of indigenous Australians.

Cathy has a tattoo which reads: "Cos I'm Free".

Probably, but I think mine might grow longer!

You must be joking! Want to hear about my favourite hero?

Is it a man, is it a boy? No, it must be another flipping female!

He's just joking!

MALALA YOUSAFZAI

Children's & Women's Rights Activist

1997–

"I am stronger than fear!"

Malala is one of the Pashtun people from Pakistan and Afghanistan.

The Taliban are followers of Islam, but have more extreme beliefs than most Muslims.

Malala wrote her blog under the name of Gul Makai, a heroine from a Pashtun folk tale.

The Taliban banned many things like make-up, kite-flying, music and films.

Malala was born on 12 July 1997, in the beautiful Swat Valley of Pakistan. When she was little it was a safe place where girls and boys ran free, flying kites and playing in the streets.

There is so much to learn and I want to learn it all.

Malala went to a school started by her father, Ziauddin. School meant everything to Malala!

"How dare the Taliban take away my basic right to education?"

Well done, Malala.

Then the Taliban took over the area and began attacking girls' schools. Malala, aged eleven and supported by her father, gave a speech on the importance of education.

Diary of a Pakistani school girl
Wednesday 14th January 2009:

--- I MAY NOT GO TO SCHOOL AGAIN ---
I was in a bad mood while going to school because winter vacations are starting from tomorrow. The principal announced the vacations but did not mention the date the school was to reopen. This was the first time this happened.

The next year, Malala, with her parents' approval, started a blog for the BBC about life under the Taliban.

The Taliban are beating people in the streets.

They will not hurt a child.

Even after Malala was revealed as the blogger, she kept speaking out for her right to education.

Don't go home yet, let's stay and chat. It might be our last day at school.

I'm too scared.

As time went on the Taliban's control of Swat increased. They destroyed more girls' schools and fewer of Malala's friends dared to attend school.

Surely, the Taliban will not harm a child - but they may hurt you Papa.

Malala was becoming well-known, and she began to receive death threats. But she was more frightened for her father, an anti-Taliban activist.

Malala makes double backflips seem a bit silly!

No, you've got to have fun!

Malala's whole family deserve a huge cheer.

But on 9 October 2012, as fifteen-year-old Malala travelled home from school, a man boarded the bus and shot her in the head. He also injured two of her friends.

Malala was alive, but in a critical condition. After undergoing surgery in Pakistan, she was flown to Birmingham in England for further treatment.

Malala received messages of support from around the world, and by March 2013 she was well enough to start school in Birmingham.

On her sixteenth birthday, Malala gave her first speech to the United Nations about children's education. Everyone applauded her bravery.

Malala and her family haven't been able to return to Pakistan and miss their beautiful homeland. Despite the Taliban's continued threats, Malala still speaks up for every child's right to quality education, equal rights for women and peace throughout the world. In October 2014, Malala became the youngest ever winner of the Nobel Peace Prize. Malala is proof that one voice of passion and truth, however young and seemingly insignificant, can be heard and can make a difference!

Malala's two friends recovered well from their injuries.

Malala's favourite colour is purple and she likes cupcakes and chocolate, but not sweets!

Malala could not have achieved any of this without her family's support.

Indian children's rights activist Kailash Satyarthi shared the Nobel Peace Prize with Malala.

HOORAY FOR LEADERS & WORLD-CHANGERS!

President of Liberia and Nobel Peace Prize winner Ellen Johnson Sirleaf (1938-) was the first female elected head of state in Africa.

Queen Elizabeth II (1926-) is the only British monarch to have reigned longer than Queen Victoria!

Dorothy Height (1912-2010) was an activist who fought for the rights of African-American women.

A teenage African-American, Claudette Colvin (1939-), had bravely refused to give up her seat nine months before Rosa, but it was Rosa who sparked the mass protests.

HATSHEPSUT
Egyptian Pharaoh
(C. 1508–1458 BC)

Egypt thrived under this noble lady's reign for over twenty years. She ruled wearing men's clothing, including the pharaoh's false beard!

ELIZABETH FRY
English Prison Reformer
(1780–1845)

Shocked by the filthy and cramped cells for women and children at Newgate Prison, Elizabeth improved conditions and organised schooling for the children and work for their mothers.

This can't go on!

QUEEN VICTORIA
Queen of the United Kingdom of Great Britain & Ireland & Empress of India
(1819–1901)

Victoria ruled for 64 years! She came to symbolise the Victorian age and its strict moral values.

EMMELINE PANKHURST
British Suffragette
(1858–1928)

VOTES FOR WOMEN

Emmeline helped found the Women's Social and Political Union, whose members fought for the right to vote and were called "suffragettes". Women over 21 got the vote in 1928.

EDITH COWAN
Australian Politician & Social Campaigner
(1861–1932)

Edith campaigned for women and children's rights. In 1921 she became the first woman to be elected to an Australian parliament.

GOLDA MEIR
Israeli Politician
(1898–1978)

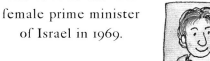

Golda was dedicated to helping displaced Jewish people, both through diplomacy and fundraising. She became the first female prime minister of Israel in 1969.

SAINT TERESA OF CALCUTTA
Albanian Nun
(1910–1997)

"Mother" Teresa dedicated her life to the poor in India. She won the Nobel Peace Prize and in 2016 she was made a saint.

"Spread love everywhere you go."

WHITES ONLY!

I've had a long day too.

ROSA PARKS
American Civil Rights Activist
(1913–2005)

In 1955, Rosa broke Alabama state law by refusing to give up her bus seat to a white person. Her arrest sparked protests which resulted in the racial segregation laws of the state being declared unconstitutional.

BARONESS BARBARA CASTLE
British Politician
(1910–2002)

Barbara introduced the Equal Pay Act in 1970 and fought for social justice, at a time when British politics was dominated by men.

KEEP BLACKBURN BOOMING!

"In politics, guts is all!"

VOTE LABOUR

These women are overwhelmingly brilliant!

No, most of them are ordinary, but do the extraordinary.

What about all the amazing women journalists who bring us news stories?

My flock has them covered - just look down below!

SIRIMAVO BANDARANAIKE
Sri Lankan Politician
(1916–2000)

"Practise simple living, decorum and dignity."

Sirimavo was the modern world's first female head of government! She was prime minister of Ceylon and Sri Lanka three times.

"Forgiveness is a virtue of the brave."

INDIRA GANDHI
Prime Minister of India
(1917–1984)

Indira was the first elected female prime minister of India. She was in power for fifteen years and her agricultural policies helped to provide food for many poor people. However not all her decisions were popular, and she was assassinated in October 1984.

American Nellie Bly (1864-1922) pioneered investigative journalism.

EDITH WINDSOR
American Activist For Lesbian, Gay, Bisexual & Transgender Rights
(1929–2017)

Edith fought for equal tax laws for partners in heterosexual and same-sex marriages.

"The way to right wrongs is to turn the light of truth upon them."

IDA B. WELLS
American Journalist & Civil Rights Activist
(1862–1931)

Ida was an investigative journalist who exposed injustices against African-Americans. Her reports revealing the violence faced by African-Americans, particularly in the south of the United States, led to her newspaper offices being attacked, but it didn't stop her being a voice against prejudice for her entire life.

Irish journalist Orla Guerin (1966-) has won many awards, including an MBE.

SHIRIN EBADI
Iranian Lawyer
(1947–)

Shirin has fought for democracy and human rights in Iran. She was also the first female judge in Iran and was awarded the Nobel Peace Prize in 2003.

"Nothing useful and lasting can emerge from violence."

DIANA, PRINCESS OF WALES
British Charity Campaigner
(1961–1997)

Diana was known as the People's Princess. She supported over 100 charities.

She was queen of our hearts!

SHERYL SANDBERG
American Executive, Activist & Author
(1969–)

Sheryl was the first woman to serve on Facebook's board of directors. She is the founder of the "Lean In Foundation" that supports women.

"Until women are as ambitious as men,

they're not going to achieve as much as men."

Kate Adie (1945-) and Lindsey Hilsum (1958-) are English journalists known for broadcasting from war zones.

MARGARET THATCHER
British Prime Minister
(1925–2013)

Margaret was the first female British prime minister. She led the country from 1979-1990.

"Don't follow the crowd, let the crowd follow you."

THANDIWE CHAMA
Zambian Children's Rights Activist
(1991–)

Thandiwe's school closed when she was eight years old. Determined to have an education, she led her classmates on a walk to find another school! She won the International Children's Peace Prize in 2007.

Sorry, we have no teachers.

CLOSED

Follow me, we'll find another school!

The English journalist Clare Hollingworth (1911-2017) was one of the first female war correspondents.

What will you do, Dot?

Just be me!

Well, that's extraordinary enough for me!

Woof!

CHARLOTTE, EMILY & ANNE BRONTË
English Writers
(1816–1855, 1818–1848, 1820–1849)

These three sisters wrote classics such as *Jane Eyre*, *Wuthering Heights* and *The Tenant of Wildfell Hall*. They wrote under pen names to disguise the fact that they were women, as only men were taken seriously as writers at this time.

HARRIET BEECHER STOWE
American Writer & Abolitionist
(1811–1896)

Harriet's novel *Uncle Tom's Cabin*, about the terrible life of an African-American slave, caught people's imaginations and helped to make the anti-slave campaign popular.

"Never give up."

ENHEDUANNA
Sumerian Poet
(2285–2250 BC)

Enheduanna is the world's first known author. She was a high priestess who wrote poetry.

BEATRIX POTTER
English Writer, Illustrator & Conservationist
(1866–1943)

Beatrix is best known for her beautifully illustrated animal stories. She taught herself to be a natural scientist, writer and illustrator.

| THE TALE OF PETER RABBIT | THE TALE OF JEMIMA PUDDLE-DUCK | THE TAILOR OF GLOUCESTER | THE TALE OF FLOPSY BUNNY |

CHIMAMANDA NGOZI ADICHIE
Nigerian Writer & Poet
(1977–)

Chimamanda is an award-winning writer who believes stories can help us to understand other people's cultures.

LOTTIE DOD
British Tennis, Hockey, Archery & Golf Star
(1871–1960)

At fifteen years old, Lottie remains the youngest woman to win the Wimbledon Ladies' Singles Championship. She also played hockey for England and won a silver Olympic medal in archery.

FANNY BLANKERS-KOEN
Dutch Athlete
(1918–2004)

Fanny was voted the greatest female athlete of the 20th century! She was a sprinter and hurdler and won four gold medals in the 1948 Olympics.

Zooooooom!

TRISCHA ZORN
American Swimmer
(1964–)

Blind from birth, Trischa is the most successful athlete ever in the Paralympic Games. She has won 41 gold, 9 silver and 5 bronze medals.

"The most important thing was to be recognised and known as a good sportsman."

JK ROWLING
English Writer
(1965–)

KING'S CROSS

Joanne is well known for her Harry Potter books. They are the best-selling series in history!

ISADORA DUNCAN
American Dancer
(1877–1927)

Isadora is known as the "Mother of Modern Dance". She broke the rigid rules of ballet, and danced in bare feet!

You want creative, just take a look at my nest!

I like the American poet, Emily Dickinson (1830-1886). Her poetry was published after her death.

I'm chirping for Yuna Kim (1990-), a South Korean figure skater. She has beaten world record scores eleven times!

Let's chirrup for Chantal Petitclerc (1969-), Canada's greatest wheelchair racer with 21 medals including 14 golds!

Chirping Beyoncé (1981-)! She's an American singer-songwriter whose hugely popular music often carries a political message.

I think I might be a dancer.

Yes, dancing's fun.

Or a jockey, they're always boys.

ANNA PAVLOVA
Russian Ballet Dancer
(1881–1931)

Anna danced with delicacy and grace, amazing audiences around the world.

MISTY COPELAND
American Ballet Dancer
(1982–)

Misty was the first African-American female principal dancer with the American Ballet Theatre.

CLARA SCHUMANN
German Musician & Composer
(1819–1896)

Clara studied music from the age of five. She played the piano and quickly gained a reputation as a child prodigy.

ARETHA FRANKLIN
American Singer, Songwriter & Musician
(1942–)

Aretha started singing aged five. She became known as the Queen of Soul for her wonderful voice.

DAME EVELYN GLENNIE
Scottish percussionist
(1965–)

Evelyn is a famous deaf percussionist, who hears and feels sound through other parts of her body.

MIRIAM MAKEBA
South African Singer & Civil Rights Activist
(1932–2008)

Miriam helped make African music popular around the world. She was exiled from South Africa after campaigning against apartheid.

MARY QUANT
Welsh Fashion Designer
(1934–)

I'm not my mother!

During the 1960s, Mary's fun fashion designs like the miniskirt and hot pants gave young people their own style. No more dressing like mum and dad!

ZAHA HADID
Iraqi-British Architect
(1950–2016)

Zaha has a worldwide reputation as one of the geniuses of contemporary architecture. She won many prestigious prizes for her extraordinary and diverse buildings.

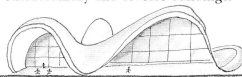

AUDREY HEPBURN
British Actress & Philanthropist
"Be happy!" (1929–1993)

Audrey is a screen legend and multiple award winner. In the late 1980s she retired from films to work for UNICEF and was later awarded the Presidential Medal of Freedom.

I'm drawing... ... *my friends!*

PAULA REGO
Portuguese Artist
(1935–)

Many of Paula's amazing prints and paintings are based on traditional fairy tales told to her by her grandmother. As a child she drew on her nursery floor!

AUGUSTA SAVAGE
American Sculptor & Civil Rights Activist
(1892–1962)

Augusta began sculpting clay animals as a child. Eventually, she won a scholarship to an art school, where she excelled. She helped to found the Harlem Artists' Guild to support other African-American artists. Augusta spent her later years teaching and inspiring others.

ELISABETTA SIRANI
Italian Painter
(1638–1665)

At a time when women were expected to be wives and mothers, Elisabetta was a successful painter and engraver by the age of seventeen! She also established an academy for other female artists.

Daddy never wanted me to be an artist.

Bravo Yuan Yuan Tan (1977–) from China, who started ballet school at eleven and has been delighting audiences ever since.

Chirrup the Indian singer Chithra (1963–). She has won lots of awards and sung like a bird in twelve languages!

I'm chirping for Bette Davis (1908–1989), a great Hollywood star and the first female president of the Academy of Motion Picture Arts and Sciences!

Nora Ephron (1941–2012) was a multi-award winning American writer, film producer and director. She fought for women's rights both in front of and behind the camera. Chirruping!

Oh no they're not! There are lots of fantastic girl jockeys.

Well, I don't suppose the horses care what gender you are!

Neigh, we don't!

HOORAY FOR SCIENTISTS, PIONEERS & ADVENTURERS!

Tweeting Marianne North (1830–1890), an English botanical artist who travelled the world painting and discovering new plants!

A chirp for Ada Lovelace (1815–1852), an English mathematician known as the first computer programmer – she was way ahead of her time!

Elizabeth Blackwell (1821–1910) was the first woman in America to become a doctor – that is a real chirrup!

Chirps for the Dutch sailor, Laura Dekker (1995–), the youngest person to circumnavigate the globe single-handed. She was sixteen and it took 518 days!

DAME JANE GOODALL
English Primatologist & Animal Rights Activist
(1934–)

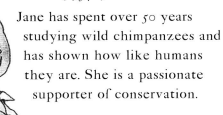

Jane has spent over 50 years studying wild chimpanzees and has shown how like humans they are. She is a passionate supporter of conservation.

BIRUTÉ GALDIKAS
Canadian Primatologist & Conservationist
(1946–)

Biruté is one of the world's leading experts on orangutans – very clever great apes with startling red hair. She works to preserve their tropical rainforest habitat.

CHARLOTTE AUERBACH
German Zoologist & Geneticist
(1899–1994)

Charlotte fled to Edinburgh from Nazi Germany. She became one of the first scientists to understand the dangers of nuclear radiation.

RITA LEVI-MONTALCINI
Italian Neurobiologist
(1909–2012)

Rita won the Nobel Prize in Physiology for her discovery of how nerve cells grow. Her work led to a better understanding of medical problems.

ROSALIND FRANKLIN
English Scientist
(1920–1958)

Rosalind's groundbreaking x-ray images helped in the discovery of the structure of DNA. DNA carries genes from one generation to the next.

ELIZABETH GARRETT-ANDERSON
English Physician & Suffragette
(1836–1917)

Elizabeth enrolled as a nurse at medical school, and after much opposition she eventually qualified as a doctor. She went on to found a hospital for women, and became the first dean of a British medical school, the first female physician in France, the first woman to be elected to an English school board and the first female mayor and magistrate in England!

"I could not live without some real work."

RACHEL CARSON
American Marine Biologist & Conservationist
(1907–1964)

Rachel's book, *Silent Spring*, challenged the use of pesticides and encouraged a global environmental movement.

SELLAPPAN NIRMALA
Indian Microbiologist
(1953–)

As a microbiology student, Sellappan discovered the first cases of the disease HIV in India. The screening and prevention programmes that followed saved lives.

GERTRUDE BELL
English Explorer, Academic, Spy, Writer & Archaeologist
(1868–1926)

"It's so nice to be a spoke in the wheel."

Gertrude explored and mapped places such as Mesopotamia and Arabia, and helped to found the modern Iraqi state. She even had an Alpine peak named after her – Gertrudspitze! At a time when most women never left home this was all highly unusual, but Gertrude was brave, intelligent and fearless!

"Did you know this is the last page of the book, Dot?"

"Yes, Abe. Sad, isn't it?"

"What shall we do now?"

What makes all these women so brave?

I don't know, maybe they just care.

EDITH CAVELL
English Nurse
(1865–1915)

As a nurse in German-occupied Belgium during the First World War, Edith risked her life by helping French and English soldiers to escape. She was finally arrested and executed.

JANE HAINING
Scottish Missionary
(1897–1944)

Jane refused to leave her school pupils, many of whom were Jewish, in Hungary during the Second World War. She stayed with them until she was arrested. She died in Auschwitz.

VLADKA MEED
Member of the Jewish Resistance in Poland
(1921–2012)

Vladka was born to a Jewish family. She pretended to be Aryan to help families escape the Nazis and to try to save them from being taken to a concentration camp.

Well, three chirps for them!

ELIZABETH KENNY
Australian Nurse
(1880–1952)

Elizabeth trained herself in nursing and travelled out into the bush to see patients. She pioneered a treatment for the disease polio, which saved many children from permanent paralysis.

JUNKO TABEI
Japanese Mountaineer
(1939–2016)

In 1975, Junko became the first woman to reach the summit of Mount Everest. She was also the first woman to climb the highest peak on every continent!

VALENTINA TERESHKOVA
Russian Astronaut
(1937–)

In 1963, Valentina, a former textile worker, became the first woman in space. She was 26 years old and orbited the earth 48 times in her spaceship Vostok 6. She logged more flight time than any astronaut who had flown before her.

And a chirrup for Amy Johnson (1903–1941), the English pilot who was the first female to fly alone from Britain to Australia!

SACAGAWEA
Lemhi Shoshone Explorer
(C. 1788–1812)

Carrying her baby, Sacagawea helped guide the famous Lewis and Clark expedition into the American West.

Humans might chirrup for American Marion Donovan (1917–1998), who invented the waterproof disposable nappy - birds don't bother with those!

 "Play is the work of the child."
MARIA MONTESSORI
Italian Physician & Educator
(1870–1952)

Maria developed an educational method that builds on how children learn through play. She opened her first Montessori school in 1907, and there are now thousands worldwide!

MARGARET KNIGHT
American Inventor
(1838–1914)

While working in a textile mill at the age of twelve, Margaret saw a fellow worker injured and came up with her first invention: a safety device for textile looms! In 1871 she received her first patent for a machine that made flat-bottomed paper shopping bags. She went on to receive over 20 patents and conceive over 100 inventions.

Maybe you could invent something?

Well birds can chirrup for American Ruth Wakefield (1903–1977), who is said to have invented the first ever chocolate chip cookie!

 "If it's a good idea, go ahead and do it!"
GRACE MURRAY HOPPER
American Computer Scientist
(1906–1992)

Grace was a Rear Admiral in the US Navy as well as a computer scientist. Her imaginative work in programming computers paved the way for non-mathematicians to use computers.

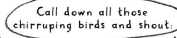 Call down all those chirruping birds and shout:

THREE CHEERS FOR WOMEN AND OTHER ASSORTED SENTIENT BEINGS!

Dear Reader,

Once upon a time I used to dream of a chocolate bar that never ended. Then, while I was writing about these truly amazing girls and women, I began to dream of a book with enough pages for every single world-changing female. Sadly, the chocolate bar never happened and the book didn't either, so I just had to choose my favourite inspirational women — I do hope you enjoyed reading about them.

These incredible females come from all backgrounds, all nations and are all ages. It is impossible to say who are the most important — it really depends on your own beliefs and interests. But I am sure that at least some of the girls and women in this book will fill you with wonder. They have certainly reminded me that, whether you are a boy or a girl, you are never too young or too old to do something world changing!

With luck and inspiration,
Marcia

QUESTION: How many women do you think I had to leave out?

ANSWER: Thousands — one of my bird friends has a list of some of them. My other bird friend has a blank banner so you can add all the women and girls that have inspired YOU — I wonder who you will add?

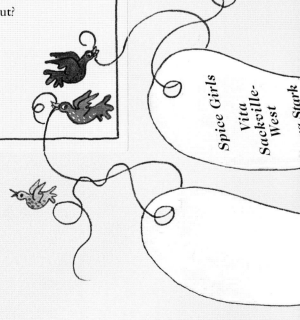

Spice Girls

Vita Sackville-West

Freya Stark

Daria

Mrs Beeton

Simone de
Beauvoir

Gwen John

Dorothy
Wordsworth

Agatha Christie

Serena Williams

Enid Blyton

Hillary
Clinton

Michelle
Obama

Princess
Anne

Elizabeth
Taylor

Marilyn
Monroe

Catherine
the Great

Maya
Angelou

Jane
Addams

Harriet
Tubman

Kate
Sheppard

Susan B.
Anthony

Olympe de
Gouges

Halet
Çambel

Jayaben Desai

Nawal El Saadawi

Germaine Greer

Billie-Jean King

Angela
Merkel

Vera
Rubin

Ireland
Manji

Oprah
Winfrey

Caitlin
Moran

Mary
Berry

The End!

Or a new
beginning!

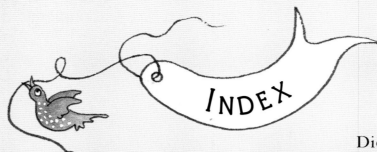

INDEX

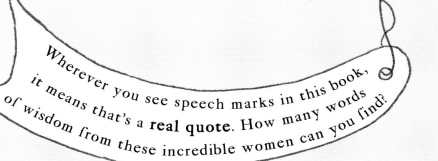

Wherever you see speech marks in this book, it means that's a **real quote**. How many words of wisdom from these incredible women can you find?

MARCIA WILLIAMS

  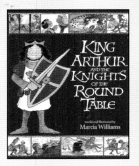 

 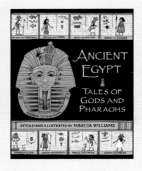 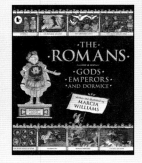 

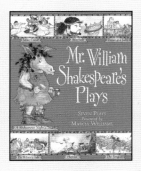  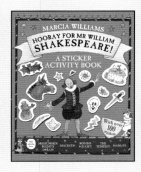 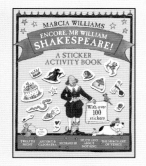

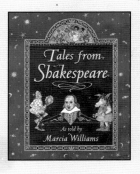 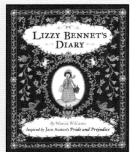  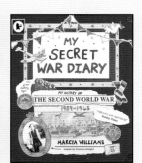

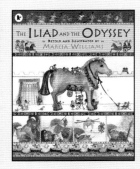 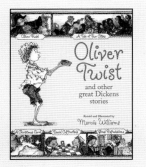  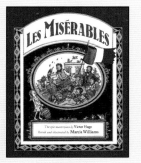

Available from all good booksellers

www.walker.co.uk